M000077096

# Secret Jewels Hidden For Discovery

By Dr. Krystal Lassiter

© 2021 By Krystal Lassiter

All Rights Reserved.

No part of this document may be reproduced or transmitted in any form by any means, electronic, mechanical, photocopying, or otherwise without prior written permission of Krystal Lassiter. All scripture quotations, unless otherwise indicated, are taken from the New King James Version Bible.

Published by Bourgeonest, LLC

Printed in the United States of America

ISBN: 978-0-578-92257-7

# Acknowledgments

Special honor and thanks to my parents, Henry and Julia Richardson, for being the best selection God could ever make as my parents. To my wonderful brother, Godchildren, grandchildren, and entire family, "Let my ceiling be your floor." Please understand, when I refer to my ceiling I am absolutely not limiting that to this book, but to my commitment to fulfill my destiny. Talena Lachelle Queen, affectionately referred to as the "word doctor," and Rev. David Riley, I appreciate your role in helping me bring this book assignment to life.

To Randall, Nigel, and Joell,
you inspire me as I hope to inspire you!

𝒦

# Contents

# Introduction

YOU DON'T HAVE TO KNOW everything, but you do have to know something — and that something is that you were born fully equipped to jump-start every successful endeavor you set your affections on.

Let me show you how to experience a life of fruitfulness and increase as a result of acknowledging and activating what's already accessible within you.

This simple yet profound book will unleash a lasting legacy that will outlive your children's children if you dare to participate.

If your goal is business, family, ministry, government, education, arts & entertainment, or simply managing yourself, this book will catapult your aspirations.

Wherever you find yourself at the start of this read, know that at this very moment, you're in your very best place for greatness.

Greatness is valuing the earth suit you're born in, then learning how to function in it with mastery.

No two people are alike on the planet, which means no one can beat you at being you.

That's intriguing!

Self-worth is a powerful discovery, yet so many people struggle in this area. True self-worth is remaining connected to your source and Creator.

Our source is God. Just like a fish must remain in the water, and flowers must remain in the earth, creation must remain in its Creator. (Romans 10: 8-10)

The process and journey for reconnecting to our Creator is different for everyone. But when you do, you'll find your true value.

The Bible says I am wonderfully and fearfully made in His image and likeness. That's powerful! (Psalm 149 & Genesis 1:26-28)

Hearing and understanding this stirs up a hunger and thirst to know God better, which results in knowing yourself better.

It's not the best practice to take your Mercedes Benz to Ford since Ford is not the designer.

If you're sick, go back to your Creator. If you're in despair and hopelessness, go back to your Creator. If you've become dull, dormant, complacent, and common, go back to your Creator.

If you feel you've been hijacked by this world — the lust of the flesh, the lust of the eyes, and the pride of life — go back to your Creator. (1 John 2:16)

~

If you're going to be infectious, you have to be certain of what you're infecting with. That's what you'll discover in this book.

Your perception, your belief, and your truth are your reality. These have been shaped by your experience and exposure, demonstrated by your routines, habits, and norms.

You can only go as far as your belief system.

What if you and I have spent all or too much time chasing the external, and not enough time pursuing the internal?

Join me in reimagining the purpose within us.

Don't stop at discovery; instead, begin distribution, which leads to dominion.

You're more than meets the eye!

Think about it.

Why would God fill us with His image and likeness and not have purposeful use for it on the earth?

Why would God say, "Occupy till I come," if He didn't give us sustainable substance to pull it off? (Luke 9)

Why would God say, "The whole earth is waiting for the sons of God to appear," if He didn't provide the value and potency in the awaited being? (Romans 8:19)

The answers to the questions are hidden in Him. And if they're hidden in Him, then it's hidden in us, since we're made in His image and likeness. God the Father, God the Son, and God the Holy Spirit are in conversation. The image and likeness referred to here is the transferable imprint of God's characteristics, which are the smallest parts of himself that equates to God.

Immediately, God declares the magnitude, outcome, and expectations of this great distribution of His characteristics: Be fruitful (produce/bring forth), multiply (reproduce again and again), fill (distribute/release), subdue (control the targeted area), and have dominion (be impactful and influential). (Genesis 1:26-28)

You and I are a walking manual of the best product ever created. Genesis 1 simply provides the instructions and model for use.

~

This book targets you to discover and/or reimagine the hidden treasures within. The following hidden jewels are embedded in the design of every person. Let's call it the *IT Factor*. These hidden treasures must be recognized and cultivated.

If you tap into these jewels, you can expect an overflow of confidence, courage, closure, confirmation, continuation, concentration, coordination, cooperation, correction, and consistency that will secure the dreams, goals, assignments, and very purpose for your life.

The following chapters start with the foundation of understanding these jewels, followed by a real-life problem that you may be facing, and ends with a real-life solution accessed through prayer.

# Jewel One: Faith

GOD CAN NEVER be put in a box. His ways are not our ways and His thoughts are not our thoughts; however, because of the deposit of His characteristics, he has made a way for us to discover who we are, through who He is: Faith!

❖ Every man has been given the measure of Faith. (Rom 12:3)

❖ Faith is the portal by which God-likeness travels between Heaven and Earth.

❖ Faith connects God to man.

❖ Faith makes the impossible, possible.

❖ Faith is potent, but it must be accessed and exerted to show results.

❖ Faith is a breath of life in dead, hopeless situations.

❖ Faith is a small substance connected to certainty and assurance in an unfailing source.

❖ Faith forces fear to fail.

❖ Faith is the solution to the problem called fear.

❖ Faith postures you in strength, courage, and victory while being surrounded by the appearance of defeat.

❖ Faith is the release of God's will in Heaven, securing every internal and external expression of His will on Earth.

❖ Faith is the spiritual equivalent of natural currency. Faith is a spiritual currency of value, just as money is a natural currency of value. My husband often says, "Money is not the most important thing, but it's right up there with breathing." In other words, our chase for money should never supersede our appetite for Faith.

❖ Faith is the synapse between immortal and eternal life. The synapse is a structure designed for passage as in the connection of the left and right hemisphere of the brain. Faith is the structure God designed as a passageway between heaven and earth.

❖ Faith can take my hidden thoughts and ideas, my seed like inclinations, and my very minute hints of possibilities, and give them life; so frame up your world! The process of framing originated from our Creator as He used His words to bring shape and form to the reality of the world we live in. (Heb 11:3)

❖ Feed your faith and starve your doubts. Your faith is fed through a continual fellowship with the Holy Spirit and the word of God.

❖ Faith is a powerful potential expressed in certainty.

# Real Life ~ Alex

**Alex:** "Nothing is going the way I intended it to go. My business is failing, right along with my marriage, and my health. If one more thing happens I will end it! My life is doing nothing but bringing hurt to everyone and everything I love."

**Counselor:** "Alex, tell me more about your business, marriage, and health."

**Alex:** "I've been married for twenty-three years. I love my wife but I had an affair early on, and I just can't seem to stop. Every time I find myself entangled in an affair she catches me. How is that even possible? She told me if I did it again, she would no longer be my woman, but I did it again. Any moment she'll confront me, and it's making me sick.

"My business involves creative systems and analytics for infrastructures. My designs targeted the in-house framework of a company and I have to be there face-to-face. So the consultations, strategy meetings, and professional development I designed aren't valuable right now as companies are reorganizing and replacing former ways of doing business. I haven't been able to meet with my clients. No meet means no meat on the table.

"To make matters worse, my doctor called me with the results of my battery of tests that my wife forced me to take. My blood pressure is high, there's a dark mass in my midsection, and my legs are acting funny. Each symptom has a long name I can't pronounce or understand. It's too much! My life is over!"

**Counselor:** "Alex, I'd say your life is just beginning."

**Alex:** "I don't know too many people who'd like to start in this mess."

**Counselor:** "Alexander, we were not promised a life of ease, but we absolutely are given options and choices. That's what wisdom is. It's the ability to know the difference. The difference in a decision, the difference in people, and a difference in a moment. Alex, you have plenty of options in front of you, but sometimes, we need others to show us. That's why the cross is both vertical and horizontal. Because we live on the earth, and we're a three-part being, we need God and man. Your view is so cloudy it's distorted your ability to make sound decisions. So let me show you what you're working with. You're aware of the signs of danger, so you have opportunity and hope. You have a good wife, so you have an opportunity for support. You have medical insurance that provides medical care for your ills. You have the ability to think, structure, and strategize your next business opportunity. And you still have life, which is another opportunity to repent and go back to the top with God and purpose. Are you willing to do the work?"

**Alex:** "Yes," he sobs.

**Counselor:** "Let's pray."

*Father, you did it again. You continue to rescue us from ourselves every time we cry out to you. You continue to make a way of escape as you've done for so many others. Holy Spirit, help Alex to think on those things that edify him, and build him up in his most holy faith. Be a fence of protection and a healer of all his dis-ease. We come into agreement that backward is not an option. As he fortifies himself in you, you will restore him anew.*

"Alex, spiritual and natural go together, so you have to do the necessary work in both areas, as we've asked God to put his super on your natural.

"I'll see you next week."

# Jewel Two: Potential

THE SUM OF GOD is *not* singular. In other words, there is no one word that could contain the fullness of who God is. Nonetheless, let's target this single transferable attribute of God: Potential!

❖ Potential is a gift from God embedded in the characteristics of mankind.

❖ Potential enables us to perform, to complete, and to establish a thing.

❖ Potential is the ability to take something from nothing and make it into something.

❖ Potential takes something from the unseen and brings it to the seen.

❖ Potential is exclusively non-exclusive and must be valued and cultivated to fruition.

❖ Potential is a hidden treasure designed to be value-added to a particular People, Place, and Thing. Not everyone will respond to your released potential. Not everyone will find value in what you bring to fruition. But

12

the moment you do, confirmation will encourage your engaged release for more.

❖ Potential is unlimited and is always potent, which means it's always full and active, never depleted, and always ready to perform.

❖ When potential is exercised, dreams, ideas, thoughts, and imaginations are materialized and maximized.

❖ When potential is realized, it leaves you in a state of success, unending supply, and unconfined solutions.

❖ Potential is a God-factor that must be released, revealed, and rendered in the earth. It's never to lie dormant, docile, disengaged, or degenerate.

❖ When potential is untapped, revelation and realization has not become your reality. When potential speaks, we must respond; since you absolutely can ignore it right to the grave, robbing the world of what could only be expressed the way you would unveil it.

❖ No one can beat you at being you. Potential can only be released the way you release it. It can only be expressed the way you express it. It can only be portrayed the way you portray it. Don't leave, stop, or abort before those awaiting your reveal — partake.

❖ Potential can be, should be, and must be, tapped, shaken, motivated, encouraged, and prompted by internal and external forces that result in uncharted, unlimited, and uninhibited possibilities.

❖ Potential must be realized, managed, and maximized.

## Real Life ~ Son

**Son:** "Dad, can I talk to you a moment?"

**Dad:** "Sure, son."

**Son:** "Dad, I'm really struggling in college. I constantly feel at war with my thoughts. I hear you saying, 'Son, you can do anything you put your mind to.' But I also hear, 'you'll never measure up, you'll never be good enough, and you're not smart enough.' When I sit in the classroom, look at television, look in the magazine, and even look in the mirror, sometimes I feel so inferior, Dad."

**Dad:** "Son, it's not uncommon to struggle with mediocrity, thoughts of low aim, and doubting your self-worth, but you better not stay there. The opportunity to wrestle between two opinions will exist for as long as you allow it. It is extremely imperative that you know Who you are and Whose you are. Remember I told you the creator of a thing provides the best manual for the use of that thing. Keep reading your manual, which is the Bible, and keep talking to your creator, which is God, your heavenly Father. The Bible reveals your potential to be creative, your potential to perform, and your potential to maximize a moment. Son, you will deliver great things to the earth. You will empty out every gift, talent, and tool God has given you to deposit. Keep saying and doing what his spirit has revealed to you.

"Let's pray, son."

*Father, I thank you that everything you started in Stephen, you are going to perform. You said you would never leave him nor forsake him. Jeremiah 29:11 says you have good thoughts toward him and you will see those thoughts to the end. I believe you are stirring up something in Stephen. You're creating a hunger and a thirst for your righteousness. You're preparing him to be contagious on his campus, his career, and every endeavor his hands and feet touch. You're going to use him as a mouthpiece and model of the potency of God expressed in mankind. Thank you for surrounding him like a shield with your favor as he walks in the confidence of your design. In Jesus' name.*

**Son:** "Thanks, Dad, I love you."

# Jewel Three: Imagination

IMAGINATION IS OFTEN referred to negative adverse thinking, but its intended use is quite the contrary.

❖ Imagination is an offspring of potential.

❖ Imagination must be tapped, which represents activation and activity; like a door, it must be opened or closed ·for accessibility and unlimited possibilities.

❖ Imagination is like a maze with unexpected turns, hurdles, and roadblocks yet succumbs to a way out. And if there is no way out, it will carve a way out.

❖ Imagination is the setting, the plot, and the ending expressed psychologically, audibly, and tangibly.

❖ Imagination decorates your thoughts with vivid intentions.

❖ Imagination goes where you take it, so keep going; exhaust every moment, every possibility, every prophecy, and every promise.

❖ Imagination gives life to dead ends, and birth to options.

❖ Imagination is the seed to a harvest of _____! (You fill in the blank.)

❖ Imagination can be confined, and encased in a lack of experience and exposure. Be sure you're not the smartest person in your circle. Be encouraged to go places and do things you've never done.

## Real Life ~ Daughter

**Daughter:** "Ever since I was a little girl, my imagination could take me places I thought my body would ever get to go. While my parents fussed, fought and made up, I'd hide in my secret closet and go as far as mind and energy would allow. Once, I was a mathematical genius like Taraji Henson in *Hidden Figures.*

"I always had a paper around so I could write the shapes and equations down. I'd imagine myself in a white lab coat or near the prettiest vast blue clear waters, but I'd always be researching, writing, teaching, creating, or speaking.

"Well, I've accomplished so much. I realize this adult brain of approximately 1350 cubic centimeters has the ability to do extraordinary things. But I can't think anymore. My drive and inspiration are gone, Momma! Daddy's gone! I don't know how other people survive the death of loved ones, but I can't, Momma! I feel so empty and lonely without him. He left too soon, Momma!"

**Mother:** "Baby, look at me. You can keep crying, you can keep telling the story, and you can even keep the moments of the good and bad memories, but you can't quit! Baby, your life's purpose is bigger than the pain you're feeling and the mistakes you'll make ahead. Robbing this world of your deposit and handing it to the grave is a mistake so many others have made. Your father would talk to me and pray to God about you all the time. He called you a gift to the world and his uniquely designed star in the universe. If somebody's talking like that about you, you must have very colorful things to do, Baby. You understand what Momma is saying to you?"

**Daughter:** "Yes ma'am."

**Mother:** "Alright, then, get some tissue, wipe your face, and let's talk to God about it.

*Father, you said the world was framed by your words. And you said the same power that raised Jesus Christ from the grave was the same power that lives in us if we confess you as Lord. So we exercise that power and ability to build Rachel up anew again. Renew her strength, fortify her heart, restore her joy, and saturate her heart and mind with a Peace that not even her smart self can understand. Release her back to the joy and passion to explore, to imagine, to create, and to establish again for your glory. Amen!*

"I'm hungry; it's time to eat, Baby!"

# Jewel Four: Decisive Language

THERE HAS TO BE A WAY to get it all out. Language is an option in the toolbox, but decisive language will always hit the intended goal.

❖ Decisive Language is a tool for pinning the bullseye.

❖ Decisive Language reveals targeted thoughts.

❖ Decisive Language gives motion to the unseen, revealed on the seen.

❖ Decisive Language forecasts what's coming, explains what is, and describes its necessity.

❖ Decisive Language is a door opener that acts as a command.

❖ Decisive Language has the ability to derail or develop.

❖ Decisive Language is unending letter formations into words; these words make up sentences, these sentences make up paragraphs, these paragraphs form chapters, these chapters form volumes, and these volumes create books of unleashed thoughts.

❖ Decisive Language is connected to your decisions, which is a key to activating the power of your brain's imaginative ability to create, carve out, and craft, which is the process for building, bridging, and bringing things forward.

❖ The wisdom in Decisive Language is knowing how to communicate with those in authority over you and those under your authority.

❖ Decisive Language is communication, and communication never stands alone. It's connected to your heart and mind, which is the origin of your language.

# Real Life ~ Crystal

**Crystal:** "There is definitely an enemy in-a-me. Most often it's easier to identify and prescribe an antidote for other people's problems before we evaluate the demons we carry.

I am acknowledging mine. It makes me doubt everything. I start off thinking I'm supposed to do this, and supposed to be there, but I can talk myself right out of it at the drop of a dime. Before you know it, I haven't done anything. I have the best excuses. My hips are too big, I stutter, I wear glasses, I don't have the money, it won't work, and my famous one, I'm afraid. This feels like a child! It takes too much of my time and body. I should be able to blame it on my weight gain. Year after year passes and I keep looking at fear growing bigger and bigger."

**Friend:** "Hey, Crystal, I'm glad you answered. I was thinking about the conversation we had last. Can we continue?"

**Crystal:** "Sure. Thanks for rescuing me."

**Friend:** "You were really talking ill of yourself."

**Crystal:** "It seems to be a recurring thing."

**Friend:** "Crystal, these words and thoughts have been like chains of bondage securing you to a life of complacency and misery. Your words and thoughts are adversely framing up your world, and it doesn't look so good. It smells and looks like stinking thinking. The results of what you're going through is represented by the words you use to describe what your life and situation will be like. You must resuscitate what you suffocated for your own well-being. Your negativity took the life out of your own life. You're basically telling God that He's really not All-Knowing and All-Powerful."

**Crystal:** "OMG!

*Lord, I repent for telling you what you made isn't good enough and what you gave isn't able enough. I thank you that I'm fashioned and designed in your likeness, and you said, 'it is good.' If you blessed it with good, then it's good. I am making a decision today that your way is perfect, and your plan is best. I destroy the boat of fear, questioning, and hesitance when you tell me what to do, what to say, and who to join in doing it. Every bondage that insulated my mind and my mouth is broken in the name of Jesus. Amen.*

**Friend:** "Thank you for obeying when you made the call. Crystal, you are absolutely a diamond in the rough."

# Jewel Five: Wisdom

BEING SKILLED AND GIFTED can create a plethora of opportunities, but wisdom is the key that can keep you in those places of opportunity.

Wisdom provides a light that allows peace and certainty to exist within you.

❖ Wisdom teaches you when to start, stop, separate, delete, and suffocate a thing.

❖ Wisdom can keep you where your gifts will take you.

❖ Wisdom is the difference between good, acceptable, and perfect. These three words are likened to measurement or portion that will accelerate you. Wisdom can determine the measure of your harvest by how well you handle or manage what you've been given.

❖ Wisdom must be honored and respected to demonstrate the value of its use. If you value it, you honor it. If you honor it, you protect it.

❖ Wisdom is the decision between temporary and long-lasting.

❖ Wisdom will extend your days of living.

❖ Wisdom gives birth to riches and honor.

❖ Wisdom is a barricade from fools and foolishness.

❖ Wisdom is a counselor, and council brings clarity and understanding.

❖ Wisdom is an automatic gain.

❖ Wisdom is a solution to your problem, if you listen.

❖ Wisdom will save you time and money, if you listen.

## Real Life ~ Susan

**Susan:** "Where did I go wrong? Drew's in jail, Kate's on her third child and no husband, and John acts like he's never leaving the house.

Being a single mother ain't no easy job. Heck, raising children ain't either. Every time I look in their faces I see him. It's not their fault, but he's not here to feel my anger, so it comes out on them. We did this to them. We instigated the cycle of abuse, poverty, and low aim. But I'm still angry and I want to blame anyone 'cause it's easier than blaming myself. I slept with the men. I partied all the time. I used drugs and alcohol. I stayed home instead of furthering my education and bettering myself. I made these detrimental decisions. I'm Susan and I'm an alcoholic. Thank you for listening."

The group responds, "Thank you for sharing."

**Meeting counselor:** "Susan, we appreciate you sharing your story. Acknowledging our part and

Confession is part of the process. The next part is a transformation that makes just as much impact as your bad decisions. I'd be glad to help you with it."

**Susan:** "I was wondering if you would pray with me?"

**Meeting counselor:** "For sure."

*Dear Lord, thank you that Susan is here with us rather than the most luxurious hospital and grave plot around. You spared her life to be a radiating center of your divine love. Wisdom is the principal thing, and you told us to ask for it. Holy Spirit, thank you for wisdom awakening in Susan. Thank you that she'll exercise it as she deciphers a difference in a moment that could change the trajectory of her life. A new scent and attraction is being released through her thinking and decisions, as her belief systems are changing and new paradigms are being formed. Moment by moment, day by day, she sets her affections in pursuit of purpose and dominion. Amen.*

# Jewel Six: Authority

AUTHORITY IS ALWAYS handed from another.

- ❖ Authority is access and approval to say and use power.
- ❖ Authority must be skillfully handled.
- ❖ Authority comes with expectations. It makes a demand on the unseen, until the unseen comes to fruition.
- ❖ Authority is like a glove or coat worn for protection, and a sign of commission.
- ❖ Authority is delegated rule; not ownership, but effective and efficient management, with the expectation to complete. (Genesis 1:28)
- ❖ Authority is executed in diligence both privately and publicly.
- ❖ Authority has guidelines that must be followed.
- ❖ Authority can be exerted both silently, audibly, and forcefully.

❖ Authority means I have the right to be present, the right to obtain, and the right to be fruitful.

❖ A person in authority doesn't have to be physically present to exercise the benefits in executing authority.

❖ Authority magnifies in capacity when exercised alongside wisdom, assurance, and humility.

❖ Authority is never a solo agent.

❖ Authority must be caught, not bought; not manipulated, not coerced, and not obtained by threat or force.

## Real Life ~ Daughter

**Daughter:** "My dad is a recovering alcoholic from over two decades of abuse, and neither my mother nor my dad went to college. This was my parents' ceiling, and my sister and my floor.

However, we never knew we lived below the poverty threshold in a family of four. The tree was always full for Christmas, the table was spread for Thanksgiving, birthdays were special, and we traveled every summer, even if it was down south with the family. Our saving grace was God's hand on us, my parents' prayer-life, and my mother's ability to manage a dollar. So of course my sister and I vowed to take as good of care for them as they did for us.

It's just so painful to witness. Taking care of someone who looks like an adult, but acts like a child can really try your patience and develop long-suffering. The financial, time, and energetic sacrifice is tremendous, but we love them. We're certain they'd do it for us time and time again, so we do what it takes to provide the best care we can to honor them. I sit in my car for a bit each time I leave to pray for them as they prayed for me.

*Father, in the name of Jesus, thank you for the long life you've given my parents, and the health, strength, and financial ability to care for them. Thank you, Lord, for hearing me as I respond in faith to your promises. I exercise the authority you've given me to push back on what's pushing me, and to subdue what tries to subdue me.*

*I am not defeated! I will complete this assignment in joy and strength! Amen.*

# Jewel Seven: Peace

WHEN YOU KNOW you've done the right thing — even when the decision is hard — it gives birth to Peace. When the task seems insurmountable but comes to fruition, it gives birth to Peace.

* ❖ Peace is an attribute of our Heavenly Father.
* ❖ Peace doesn't just come at the end, it's actually intertwined in the assurance of what you're called to do, if you tap into it.
* ❖ Peace is a product of obedience.
* ❖ Peace is a fruit of focus and diligence.
* ❖ Peace is an unseen presence that we can carry through the most hellish situation. It causes people to ask the question how, while we await the opportunity to tell them WHO.
* ❖ Peace is the result of confidently hearing, confidently speaking, and confidently doing something you are sure to complete.
* ❖ Peace is an assurance of what was, what is, and what will be.
* ❖ Peace is safety, and safety is Rest.

❖ Peace is trusting in the mechanism that can take you from one place to the right place.

❖ Peace is contagious. The characteristics of God are so delicious, others will desire a bite of it.

❖ Since so many other things fight for your space of Peace, Peace must be accepted, pursued, and guarded.

❖ Peace has enemies named poverty, anxiety, and fear. They are always contending for the seat of Peace. You must decide on Peace as the winner, daily.

❖ Peace is an incredible aura that extends before you, in you, under you, and around you.

## Real Life ~ Momma

*No Justice! No Peace! No Justice! No Peace!*
*No Justice! No Peace!*

**Mother:** "I wake up in hot alarming sweat each night to these chants. I want my baby back! They took him from me. I can't get his voice out of my head, and I don't want his face to be erased. It just ain't right. I can't take it anymore!"

**Daughter:** "Momma, if you don't learn to channel your rage and feelings of helplessness, it will kill you. We can't lose you, too."

~ later ~

**Daughter:** Momma went from repeated crying to silence, and then she finally came out of her room with such a glow of confidence. She sat my brother and me down for a talk.

**Mother:** "We are a family. We will remember your brother as an activist. This family has been called to bridge gaps: gaps between ethnicity and race, gaps in economics, gaps in health care, and gaps in quality education. Sandra, you have the gift of communication and influence. We're going to target you in the area of political science and law. Terrance, you have the gift of numbers and systems. We'll target you to finance, real estate, and banking. Both of you will use your gifts and favor to open doors of access for yourself and others while closing gaps that exist. If you manage what God gives you, He will entrust you with plenty. Let's present our plans to the Lord."

**Son:** "We're in agreement, Momma."

**Mother:** *Lord, you said if two or three are in agreement, you would be in our midst. Thank you for giving this family something we can understand, even in the midst of our pain and suffering. You have sprung up a well of vision, hope, peace, and joy. Holy Spirit you've activated a reservoir of confidence to establish a legacy of bridging gaps in our children's children. Thank you for the provisions that accompany this journey. Amen.*

# Conclusion

YOU ARE A GIFT to the earth.

Don't let anything, not even YOU, stop you from emptying out every purposeful intention, divine assignment, destiny pursuit, gift, talent, or idea within you.

Did you know that no one can beat you at being you? You are a designer's original. The world is waiting for your unique reveal. Your deposit in the earth is one-of-a-kind. But we'll never know your deposit in the earth if it's never unleashed.

This book of jewels is assigned to jump start, uncap, and ignite your ability to pursue. These jewels will catapult your good to better, and your better to best. It's never too early, and certainly not too late!

The seven Jewels of Faith, Potential, Imagination, Decisive Language, Wisdom, Authority, and Peace are treasured possessions hidden within us. They're not hidden to prevent discovery; rather, they're hidden because of their value. Jewels are delicate and precious, as they also have a high worth that draws attention by its sparkle.

Release your sparkle as you manage the jewels within you.

# Bible Reference Page

**Romans 10:9-10** ~ that if you confess with your mouth the Lord Jesus and believe in your heart that God has raised Him from the dead, you will be saved. For with the heart one believes unto righteousness, and with the mouth confession is made unto salvation.

**Psalm 139:14** ~ I will praise You, for [a]I am fearfully *and* wonderfully made; Marvelous are Your works, And *that* my soul knows very well

**Genesis 1:26-28** ~ Then God said, "Let Us make man in Our image, according to Our likeness; let them have dominion over the fish of the sea, over the birds of the air, and over the cattle, over [a]all the earth and over every creeping thing that creeps on the earth." So God created man in His *own* image; in the image of God He created him; male and female He created them. Then God blessed them, and God said to them, "Be fruitful and multiply; fill the earth and subdue it; have dominion over the fish of the sea, over the birds of the air, and over every living thing that [b]moves on the earth."

**1John 2:16** ~ For all that *is* in the world—the lust of the flesh, the lust of the eyes, and the pride of life—is not of the Father but is of the world.

**Rom 12:3** ~ For I say, through the grace given to me, to everyone who is among you, not to think *of himself* more highly than he ought to think, but to think soberly, as God has dealt to each one a measure of faith

**Heb11:3** ~ By faith we understand that the [a]worlds were framed by the word of God, so that the things which are seen were not made of things which are visible

**Jeremiah 29:11** ~ For I know the thoughts that I think toward you, says the Lord, thoughts of peace and not of evil, to give you a future and a hope.

# About the Author

KRYSTAL FAYE LASSITER is a champion and dedicated supporter of women in their assignment as influencers, strategists, innovators, communicators, decision-makers, and shapers of destiny. Her unwavering devotion to empowering others spiritually and academically is an outstanding contribution to her community far and near for over twenty years. She is a master teacher, the director and founder, along with her husband, Dr. Randall Lassiter, of the former Future Scholars Learning Center, in Paterson, New Jersey, and partner in ministry with her husband and senior pastor of Calvary Baptist Church, Paterson, New Jersey.

Her professional career, volunteer engagement, and benevolent fervor align deeply with her mission of strengthening the family.

A true advocate for children, Krystal is dedicated professionally and personally to making sure children in her sphere of influence have the opportunity to be successful in their academic pursuits and in life as value-added world-changers as she leads by example, graduating from Seton Hall University, South Orange, New Jersey, Dr. Krystal Lassiter, Ed.D.

With humor, a strategic mind, and a humble and imperturbable demeanor, Krystal provides an infectious tenacity as a leader.

She is permanently married to Randall Lassiter, and has two sons, Nigel Stephen and Joell Alexander.

To contact Dr. Krystal Lassiter:
InfoKrystalLassiter@gmail.com